WHAT'S THAT I HEAR?

Adam Bellamy

Enslow Publishing
101 W. 23rd Street
Suite 240
New York, NY 10011
USA
enslow.com

Published in 2018 by Enslow Publishing, LLC.
101 W. 23rd Street, Suite 240, New York, NY 10011

Library of Congress Cataloguing-in-Publication Data

Names: Bellamy, Adam, author.
Title: What's that I hear? / Adam Bellamy.
Description: New York, NY : Enslow Publishing, 2018. | Series: All about my senses | Audience: Pre-K to grade 1. | Includes bibliographical references and index.
Identifiers: LCCN 2017002289| ISBN 9780766086036 (library-bound) | ISBN 9780766087958 (pbk.) | ISBN 9780766087965 (6-pack)
Subjects: LCSH: Hearing—Juvenile literature. | Senses and sensation—Juvenile literature.
Classification: LCC QP462.2 .B45 2018 | DDC 612.8/5—dc23
LC record available at https://lccn.loc.gov/2017002289

Printed in the United States of America

To Our Readers: We have done our best to make sure all websites in this book were active and appropriate when we went to press. However, the author and the publisher have no control over and assume no liability for the material available on those websites or on any websites they may link to. Any comments or suggestions can be sent by email to customerservice@enslow.com.

Photo Credits: Cover, p. 1 Blake Little/The Image Bank (girl with headphones), Flavio Edreira/EyeEm/Getty Images (background); lilam8/Shutterstock.com (spine graphic); p. 3 (left), 10 wavebreakmedia/Shutterstock.com; p. 3 (center), 20 adriaticfoto/Shutterstock.com; p. 3 (right), 8 Dwight Smith/Shutterstock.com; p. 4 FatCamera/E+/Getty Images; p. 6 chartphoto/Shutterstock.com; p. 12 perqsista/iStock/Thinkstock; p. 14 Olivia Bell Photography/Moment Open/Getty Images; p. 16 Irwan Bujang/Shutterstock.com; p. 18 Lester Balajadia/Shutterstock.com; p. 22 VaLiza/iStock/Thinkstock.

Contents

Words to Know

headphones   sign language   siren

Hearing is an important sense. I use my ears to hear.

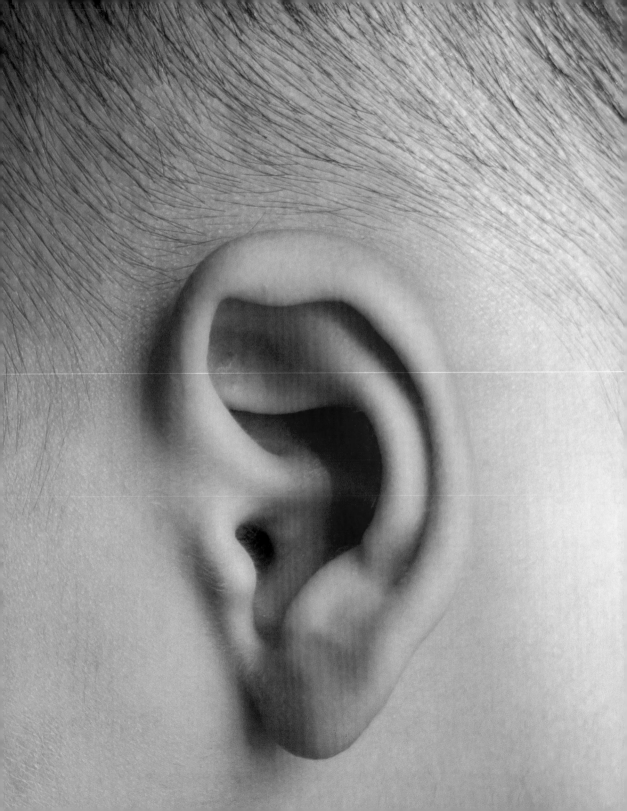

The part of my ear I can see is not my whole ear. Most of my ear is inside my head.

Hearing lets me know about danger. When I hear a police siren, something bad may have happened.

My ears can also hear music. I use headphones to listen to my favorite songs.

Why do dogs bark? Dogs bark to let me know they hear something, too!

Listen to the cat purr.
She is happy.

When I hear thunder, I know that lightning will come soon.

I can hear the wind outside during a storm. It sounds like it is howling!

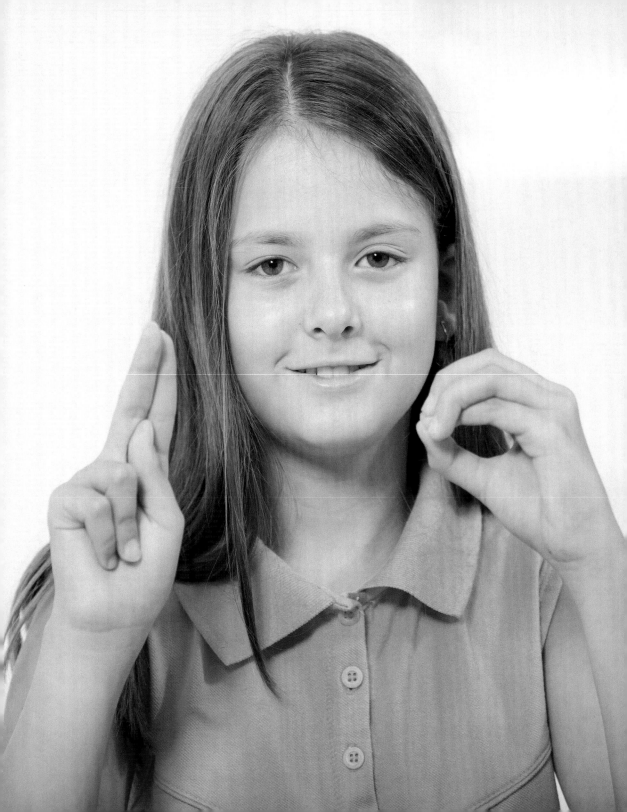

Some people cannot hear.
They use their hands
to speak and their eyes to
listen. This is called sign
language.

If I cup my hand around my ear, I can hear even better! I hear many different sounds every day!

Read More

Issa, Joanna. *What Can I Hear?* Portsmouth, NH: Heinemann, 2014.

Murray, Julie. *I Can Hear.* Minneapolis, MN: Abdo Kids, 2015.

Wheeler-Toppen, Jodi Lyn. *Our Ears Can Hear.* North Mankato, MN: Capstone Press, 2017.

Websites

ABCYa.com
  www.abcya.com/five_senses.htm
  Fun cartoons help you learn about your senses.

Science for Kids
  www.scienceforkidsclub.com/senses.html
  Learn more about the senses.

Index

Guided Reading Level: B
Guided Reading Leveling System is based on the guidelines recommended by Fountas and Pinnell.

Word Count: 153